THE
PEPPER PANTRY:
Chipotles

*Dave DeWitt
and Chuck Evans*

CELESTIAL ARTS
Berkeley, California

Celestial Arts
an imprint of Ten Speed Press
Post Office Box 7123
Berkeley, California 94707
www.tenspeed.com

Distributed in Australia by Simon & Schuster Australia, in Canada by Ten Speed Press Canada, in New Zealand by Southern Publishers Group, in South Africa by Real books, and in the United Kingdom and Europe by Publishers Group UK.

Design by Toni Tajima
Cover photograph by Jonathan Chester

Library of Congress Cataloging-in-Publication Data:
DeWitt, Dave
  The pepper pantry. Chipotles / by Dave DeWitt and Chuck Evans
        p.   cm.
  Includes bibliographical references
  ISBN-13: 978-0-89087-828-6 / ISBN-10: 0-89087-828-5
  1. Cookery (Hot peppers) 2. Hot peppers. I. Evans, Chuck.
II. Title
  TX803.P46D488   1997
  641.6'384—dc20
                                                    96-30488
                                                    CIP

Printed in Malaysia
6   7   8   –   11   10   09   08

CONTENTS

· iii ·

INTRODUCTION

Both of us got acquainted with chipotle chiles during our frequent visits to Mexico. After all those years of tasting Mexican chiles, the chipotle still stands out because of its unique combination of smokiness and heat. Chuck became so enamored of the chipotle that he designed several chipotle sauces for his company, Sauces and Salsas, Ltd. His Montezuma® brand of smokey chipotle hot sauces and salsas is one of only two products to have trademarks of variety names of chiles; the other, of course, is Tabasco® Sauce.

As we point out, chipotle is a generic term for any smoked chile and usually means the smoked red jalapeño. However, there are other varieties of smoked chiles available, ranging from the diminutive coban to the long pasilla oaxaqueño to the blistering smoked habanero. For adventurous chileheads, we have included instructions for smoking your own chipotles.

Simply put, the recipes are our personal favorites of the dozens and dozens that we've tasted over the years. We offer quite a few sauces because that is the most common use for chipotles in both Mexico and the rest of North America. The chipotle sauces are used in cooking or as a condiment, just like any other sauce or salsa. Sauces are a great way to intensify the smoky chipotle experience.

The only other book on chipotles that we're aware of is *Chipotle Chile Cookbook* (The Olive Press) by our friend Jackie McMahan, and we recommend it highly.

THE
SMOKY CHILES

Nomenclature

Generally speaking, in English "chipotle" refers to any smoked chile pepper. The Spanish word *chipotle* is a contraction of *chilpotle* in the Náhuatl language of the Aztecs, where *chil* referred to the hot pepper and *potle* was derived from *poctli*, meaning smoked. The word was apparently reversed from Náhuatl, where it originally was spelled *pochilli*. Other early spellings in Mexico are *tzilpoctil*, *tzonchilli*, and *tex-ochilli*.

The most commonly smoked chiles are jalapeños, named for the city of Jalapa in the state of Veracruz. They are also known in Mexico as *cuaresmeños*, or Lenten chiles. In Puebla, Central Mexico, and Oaxaca, jalapeños are known as *huachinangos*, while in coastal Mexico and Veracruz they are called *chiles gordos*.

Origins

Smoked chiles had their origin in the ancient civilization of Teotihuacan, north of present-day Mexico City. It was the largest city/state in Mesoamerica, and flourished centuries before the rise of the Aztecs. Chipotles also made an appearance in the marketplaces of Tenochtitlán, the capital city of the Aztecs that is now called Mexico City. Certain varieties of fleshy chiles, now called jalapeños, would not dry properly in the sun—their thick flesh would rot first. However, like meats, they could be preserved by the process known as smoke-drying.

History

Bernardino de Sahagún, a Spanish friar who lived in Mexico in the early 1500s, described a dish called *teatzin*, which was served in Cholula in the state of Puebla. It contained a combination of chipotle and pasilla sauces for stewing fresh jalapeños and lenten palm flowers.

In 1575, a Spanish visitor to Mexico, Juan de la Cueva, described a dish that combined the seedless chipotles (*capones*), onions, pine nuts, and a broth with meat juice and *pulque* (agave beer). The sauce was simmered with chunks of meat to create *pipián de piñon*.

For hundreds of years after the Aztecs, smoked chiles were found predominantly in the markets of Central and South Mexico, such as Puebla, Oaxaca, Veracruz, and Chiapas. In Huatasco in the state of Veracruz, a salsa made with tomatoes, peanuts, and chipotles has been made for centuries. It is called *tlatonile* (page 33).

Varieties

The true chipotle is tan to brown, leathery, and is often described as looking like a cigar butt. It is deeply imbued with smoke and is both hot and flavorful. This main variety is also called *chile ahumado* (smoked chile); *chile meco* (blackish-red chile; *meco* is close to *seco*, meaning dry); the double terms *chipotle meco* and *chipotle típico*, and just *típico*. Further confusing the issue is a cultivated variety of jalapeño that is also named 'Típico.' Yes, the 'Tipico' variety is often smoked to become a *típico chipotle*.

Other varieties of smoked jalapeños are often mistaken for the típico chipotle. The most common one is called *morita*, which means "little blackberry" in Spanish. The color of this smoked chile is dark red, sometimes approaching purple in color. Often the morita is referred to as a smoked serrano chile, but this is inaccurate. Both the típico and the morita are smoked jalapeños; the difference is that the morita is not smoked nearly as long, and thus it remains very leathery and pliable. Not only is the smoky flavor much more intense in the típico, its flavor is much richer.

But the morita is commonly marketed as the típico chipotle because it can bring two to four dollars more per pound with that name. Unfortunately, most of the "chipotles" being sold in markets in the United States are in actuality the inferior moritas. This is because most of chipotles produced in Mexico are eaten there, leaving little for export.

To make up for lack of the típico variety to export, producers in the northern states of Mexico, particularly Chihuahua, have turned to the moritas, which are much less expensive to produce. Unfortunately, they call the moritas "chipotles" and sometimes claim that they have never heard of the típico variety. To further confuse the issue, in the interior the típico is known by brokers as "Veracruz."

Other varieties of smoked chiles include:

—*Cobán*: a piquín chile that is smoked in southern Mexico and Guatemala.

—*Pasilla de Oaxaca*: a variety of pasilla chile that is smoked in Oaxaca and is used in the famous *mole negro*.

—*Jalapeño chico*: jalapeños that are smoked while they're still green. Usually, they are culls from the fresh market that need to be preserved.

—*Capones:* This rare smoked chile is a red jalapeño without seeds; the term means "castrated ones." They are quite expensive and are rarely exported.

—*Habanero:* A smoked habanero product has been introduced as a very hot substitute for chipotles.

Heat scale

Of course, the heat scale of smoked chiles varies considerably. The cobán and habaneros are the hottest of the smoked chiles and the morita and típico are the mildest. Jalapeños retain their heat level when they're smoked, which ranges from about 5,000 to 10,000 Scoville heat units, measured in the dried form. By comparison, New Mexican chiles are typically 500 to 1,000 Scoville heat units, and habaneros range from 80,000 to more than 300,000. When many chipotles are added to a dish, the result can be quite pungent.

FROM SEED
TO SHELF

The jalapeño, the main variety of chile that is smoked, is named after the city of Jalapa in Mexico (where it is no longer grown). The jalapeño is probably the most famous chile pepper in Mexico and the United States. Many people enjoy growing jalapeños and find that their own garden is the only reliable source for red jalapeños, which are preferred for smoking.

Botanical description

The plant grows from 2 to 3½ feet tall; however, one grower in Jacksonville, Florida, has a jalapeño measuring 12 feet, 3 inches tall. The jalapeño has a compact single stem or upright multibranched habit, and has light to dark green foliage. The flower corollas are white with no spots. The pods, which are conical and cylindrical, are pendant and

about 1½ to 2½ inches long and ¾ inch
to 1 inch wide. They are green (occasionally sunlight will cause purpling), maturing
to red, and the yield is twenty-five to thirty-five
fruits per plant.

Cultivation

Home gardeners should remember that the United
States varieties of jalapeños flourish better in semi-
arid climates—ones with dry air combined with
irrigation. If planted in hot and humid zones in the
United States during the summer, the yield
decreases; thus the Mexican varieties such as
'Típico' should be grown instead. The growing
period is a minimum of eighty days from trans-
planting.

More than forty thousand acres of jalapeños are
grown in Mexico, but considerably fewer are cultivated in the U.S., mostly in Texas and New
Mexico. In Mexico, the primary growing regions
are the states of Veracruz, Oaxaca, and Chihuahua,
where most of the crop is exported to the United

States. Other growing regions are the states of Jalisco, Sonora, Sinaloa, and Chiapas in Mexico, the southwestern United States, and Costa Rica.

Recommended varieties

'Early Jalapeño'—very hot, fruits early

'Jalapa Hot'—hybrid; medium-hot pods

'Jalapeño M'—large, dark green, hot pods

'Mitla'—large, hot, early pods

'TAM Mild'—medium sized, mild pods

Post-harvest use

Most jalapeños from the home garden are used fresh in salsas, sliced into rings for nachos, or pickled for later use. Jalapeños are commonly used in both homemade and commercial salsas and picante sauces.

About 20 percent of the jalapeño crop in

Mexico is turned into chipotles.
Another 20 percent of the crop is eaten in
the fresh form, and the remaining jalapeños
are processed or pickled.

Smoking

Why did Native Americans smoke chiles in the
first place? Perhaps some thick-fleshed chiles such
as early jalapeños were dropped near the commu-
nal fire and later a leathery, preserved chile was
the result. Since smoking is believed (along with
salting) to be one of the earliest preservation
methods, it would make sense that the "meaty"
chiles could be smoked right along with the meat.

In the town of Delicias in northern Mexico, the
red jalapeños are smoked in a large pit on a rack
that can be made out of wood, bamboo, or metal.
Another nearby pit contains the fire and is con-
nected to the smoking pit by an underground tun-
nel. The pods are placed on top of the rack where
drafts of air pull the smoke up and over the pods.
A farm may have a smoker of a different design at

the edge of the fields—a fireplace of bricks with grates at the top and a firebox below. This smoker is for small batches.

Chipotles smoked in this manner are not always available north of Mexico. And with prices of chipotles topping fifteen dollars per pound when they are available, an attractive alternative is for cooks to smoke their own. As chile expert Paul Bosland of New Mexico State University commented in an article in *Chile Pepper* magazine, "It is possible to make chipotle in the backyard with a meat smoker or Weber-type barbecue with a lid. The grill should be washed to remove any meat particles because any odor in the barbecue will give the chile an undesirable flavor. Ideally, the smoker or barbecue should be new and dedicated only to smoking chiles." The result of this type of smoking is a chipotle that more resembles the red morita than the classic tan-brown típico.

There are five keys to achieving a high quality in homemade chipotles: the maturity and quality of the pods, the moisture in the pods, the type of wood used to create the smoke, the temperature of the smoke drying the pods, and the amount of time the fruits are exposed to the smoke and heat. But remember that smoking is an art, so variations are to be expected and even desired.

Recommended woods are fruit trees or other hardwoods such as hickory, oak, and pecan. Pecan is used extensively in parts of Mexico and in southern New Mexico to flavor chipotle. Although mesquite is a smoke source in Mexico, we prefer the less greasy hardwoods. Mesquite charcoal (not briquets) is acceptable, however, especially when soaked hardwood chips are placed on top to create even more smoke. It is possible, however, that the resinous mesquite smoke (from the wood, not charcoal) contributes to the tan brown coloration of the típico variety of chipotle.

Wash all the pods and discard any that have insect damage, bruises, or are soft, and remove the stems from the pods. Start two small fires on each side of the barbecue bowl, preferably using one of the recommended hardwoods. If you are using a meat smoker with a separate firebox, simply build the fire in the firebox.

Place the pods in a single layer on the grill rack so they fit between the two fires. For quicker smoking, cut the pods in half lengthwise and remove the seeds. Keep the fires small and never directly expose the pods to the fire, which will cause them to dry unevenly or burn. The intention is to dry the pods slowly while flavoring them with smoke. If you are using charcoal briquets, soak hardwood chips in water before placing them on the coals so the wood will burn slower and create more smoke. The barbecue vents should be opened only partially to allow a small amount of air to enter the barbecue, thus preventing the fires from burning too fast and creating too much heat.

Check the pods, the fires, and the chips hourly and move the pods around, always keeping them away from the fires. It may take up to forty-eight hours to dry the pods completely, which means that your fire will probably burn down during the night and will need to be restoked in the morning. When dried properly, the pods will be hard, light in weight, and brown in color. After the pods have dried, remove them from the grill and let them cool. To preserve their flavor, place them in an airtight, plastic bag.

Ten pounds of fresh jalapeños yield just one pound of chipotles after the smoking process is complete. But a pound of chipotle goes a long way, as a single pod is usually enough to flavor a dish.

A quick smoking technique involves drying red jalapeños (sliced lengthwise, seeds removed) in a dehydrator or in an oven with just the pilot light on. They should be desiccated but not stiff. Then smoke them for three hours over fruitwood in a traditional smoker with a separate firebox, or in the Weber-style barbecue as described above. This technique separates the drying from the smoking so you spend less time fueling the smoker.

Chuck has experimented with smoke-drying pods on a large scale with jalapeños grown near Toledo, Ohio. The large, red pods had a lot of white "corking," which is a desirable trait for jalapeños in Mexico. Thus they resembled the variety called 'Huachinango.'

He took the pods to a local catering firm that specialized in barbecue, and used one of their revolving rack smokers. With hickory wood as his smoke source, he smoked the pods at 110 degrees for three days. He was attempting to duplicate the típico variety but the result was much more like the mora or morita, with their bright, red-brown, leathery appearance.

The second attempt at duplicating the típico variety was in a meat-packing plant in a modern room with climate-controlled, injected smoke. The result was identical to the first try.

Then Chuck repeated the experiment a third time with a primitive smoker in a sausage-making facility. It was a small room with racks set on the ground and smoke that continuously circulated. He left the pods in the room for a week, and the chipotles were closer to the desired tan-brown color, but the pods still had too much moisture in them. He concluded that the raw red jalapeños contained extra moisture to begin with.

Obviously, the Mexicans have perfected the típico technique, while we Americans are struggling to duplicate it with more modern equipment. There is a delicate balance between the pit temperature, the amount and type of smoke, and the length of time that is needed to produce the perfect chipotle. Perhaps we should dig smoking pits in our backyards and begin growing mesquite trees.

Smoking habaneros

Our friend Rob Polishook is one of the owners of Chile Today–Hot Tamale, a company that introduced the Smoked Habanero™ chiles to American chileheads. When we asked him about his technique for smoking the hottest chiles in the world, he wouldn't reveal his specific trade secrets, but he did give us some general techniques.

"Producing the smoked habanero chile is an intricate and time-consuming process," he wrote. "The habaneros are smoked over a medley of exotic woods, herbs, and spices. The habaneros are smoked for sixteen to thirty hours and must be turned and sorted depending on their density and size at least once an hour. This process ensures that the habaneros do not burn and will have a rich, smoky, citrus, incendiary flavor. Chile Today–Hot Tamale's homemade habanero smoker has smoked thousands of pounds of habaneros. Similar to a chef's favorite pan, it has seasoned perfectly." Rob's final comment is good evidence for devoting a smoker strictly to chipotles.

Storage

Many cooks have had success storing chipotles in an airtight, plastic bag in a cool and dry location. If humidity is kept out of the bags, the chipotle will last for twelve to twenty-four months. A more secure method to store them at room temperature is to keep them in glass jars with tight-fitting, rubber-sealed tops.

Of course, the best storage of all is to freeze them. Use heavy-duty freezer bags and double-bag the chipotles. They will keep for years with no noticable loss of flavor or smoke.

Making chipotle powder

A "dried" chipotle usually has about 80–90 percent of its moisture removed, which is enough, with the smoke, to preserve it and retard bacterial growth but not enough to create a powder. Therefore, regardless of whether you are using the típico chipotle or the morita, the chiles must be further dried in a food dehydrator or in the oven on the lowest possible heat until they are so dry that you can snap them in half.

Put on a painter's mask to protect you from uncontrollable sneezing, and break the chipotles into manageable pieces. Use an electric spice mill or a coffee grinder to reduce the pod pieces to a powder.

Because the chiles are so desiccated,
the chipotle powder stores well in air-tight
containers such as small jars. But remember,
powders will oxidize and absorb odors from the
air or the freezer, so if you intend to freeze the
powders or store them in bags at room temperature, triple-bag them first.

Commercial products

In the United States and Canada, dried chipotles
are usually sold in the típico or morita forms. They
are available from mail-order sources (page 86).

Chipotles en Adobo, a tomato-based vinegar
sauce, is manufactured by the major Mexican spice
and sauce companies, including San Marcos, La
Preferida®, Embasa, Herdez®, and La Costeña. In
this form, the chipotles have rehydrated and have
been flavored by the sauce. For cooks wishing to
duplicate this method of preservation, we have
provided a recipe for Chipotles Adobados (Chipotle
Chiles in Adobo Sauce), page 30.

Manufacturers of salsas and hot sauces contain-

ing chipotles include Búfalo® Chipotle
Hot Sauce, Montezuma® Smokey
Chipotle® Hot Sauce and Smokey Chipotle®
Salsa, Don Alfonso Chipotles en Adobo, El Paso
Chile Company, Del Monte, La Preferida®, San
Angel, and Coyote Cocina.

CHIPOTLES IN THE KITCHEN

Flavor elements

Chef and author Mark Miller described the flavor of chipotles in one of his books as "smoky and sweet in flavor with tobacco and chocolate tones, a Brazilnut finish, and a subtle, deep, rounded heat." In another book, he added "leather, coffee, and mushrooms" as flavor components. We believe that smoked jalapeños are much more interesting and flavorful than the fresh ones.

Rehydrating chipotles

Unless you are going to make powder, both the típico and morita varieties of chipotles will need to be rehydrated. Bring a pot of water to a boil, turn off the heat, and add the chipotles. Depending upon their degree of desiccation, the chiles should absorb water and be fully hydrated between thirty and sixty minutes. The left-over water, which will have some flavor, can be used in chipotle sauces. Usually, after rehydrating, the seeds and stems are removed before the chiles are used in a recipe.

Canned chipotles

Chipotles canned in *adobo* sauce are already rehydrated, and, of course, are flavored by the tomato-based sauce. Cooks must decide whether or not to rinse off the chipotles to remove most the tomato flavor, or to use the chipotles with the sauce.

Using chipotle powder

Powdered chipotles are used just like any other chile powder. The powder, if properly stored, retains its smoky flavor and is great for use in rubs for smoked meats, in sauces, and in chili con carne. Remember that the chipotle powder will be much hotter than red chile powder made with New Mexican chiles, and hotter than commercial "chili" powder that has other spices added. Substitute one teaspoon chipotle powder for each chipotle called for in the recipe.

Other substitutions

Any smoked chile pod, sauce, paste, or powder may be substituted for any other. Remember, generally speaking, the smaller the chile, the hotter it is, so cobans will be hotter than moritas, and moritas hotter than pasillas de Oaxaca. The only exception is the smoked habanero, which is larger and hotter than the coban.

When substituting sauces for chipotle pods, an approximate equivalent is one tablespoon of sauce per pod. Some cookbooks recommend cayenne hot sauce mixed with liquid smoke as a substitute, but we find this to be inferior to the real thing.

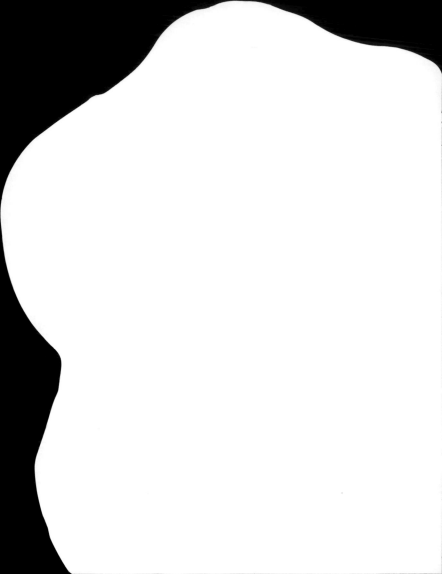

Sauces, salsas, condiments, and a drink

CHIPOTLES ADOBADOS

(Chipotle Chiles in Adobo Sauce)

YIELD: ABOUT 1½ QUARTS   HEAT SCALE: HOT

Here's a pickled chile recipe from Tlaxcala. These sweet-hot pickled chiles can be the basis of a sauce of their own if they're further puréed, or they can be served as a condiment with enchiladas and other main dishes. Note that this recipe requires advance preparation.

½ pound dried chipotle chiles, stems removed
1 quart vinegar
1 head garlic, peeled and crushed
½ cup *piloncillo*, or ½ cup packed brown sugar
1 cup roasted and peeled green chile, such as
    poblano or New Mexican
2 medium tomatoes, chopped
6 black peppercorns
3 bay leaves
1 teaspoon ground cumin
Salt to taste

Soak the chipotles in water until they rehydrate, at least an hour, then drain.

In a saucepan, add ½ of the vinegar, ½ of the garlic and the brown sugar. Cook this mixture for about 20 minutes, then add the chipotles.

In another pan, combine the green chile, tomatoes, remaining garlic, peppercorns, bay leaves, cumin, remaining vinegar, and salt to taste. Cook for about 30 minutes, covered, over medium heat. Add the chipotle chile mixture, stir well, and store in sterilized jars.

PASTA DE CHIPOTLE
(Chipotle Paste)

YIELD: ABOUT 2 CUPS   HEAT SCALE: HOT

Pasta *is the Spanish word for paste, not macaroni. This paste, which keeps well in the refrigerator for a couple of weeks, is added to soups and salsas and to vinaigrette dressings to perk up the flavor of the dish. It's also great as a marinade or basting sauce for roasts, ribs, chicken breasts, and shrimp.*

2 cans chipotle chiles in adobo or 2 cups
 Chipotles Adobados (page 30)
2 tablespoons corn oil
4 cloves garlic
1 teaspoon Mexican oregano
1 teaspoon ground cumin
1 teaspoon thyme
1 teaspoon black pepper

Combine all ingredients in a blender or food processor and purée. Transfer to a clean jar, cover, and store in the refrigerator.

TLATONILE

(Tomato-Peanut Salsa)

YIELD: ABOUT 2½ CUPS   HEAT SCALE: MEDIUM

This salsa comes from the village of Huatasco in the state of Veracruz. It makes a tasty sauce for grilled or roasted meats and poultry. The recipe was collected from an old cookbook of Veracruz-area recipes.

5 to 6 ripe tomatoes, diced
¼ cup minced white onion
¼ cup peanuts, chopped
1 to 2 chipotle chiles en adobo, finely chopped
Juice of ½ fresh lime
Salt to taste
6 to 10 sprigs cilantro, chopped

Combine all the ingredients thoroughly and serve chilled. This makes a wonderful dipping sauce for tortilla chips. You may also serve as a condiment for beef kebabs.

CHUCK'S CHIPOTLE SAUCE

YIELD: ABOUT 3 CUPS   HEAT SCALE: HOT

This is a version of Chuck's number-one brown hot sauce, Smokey Chipotle Hot Sauce®, which he manu-factures under the Montezuma brand. If dried chipotle chiles are available, place them in a bowl and cover them with distilled vinegar. After several days, the chiles will be reconstituted and plump. Note that this recipe requires advance preparation.

12 reconstituted chipotle chiles
1 medium onion, chopped
3 cloves garlic, sliced
3 cups water
¼ cup cider vinegar
¼ cup tomato sauce
Salt to taste
2 cups white distilled vinegar (or more or less)

Place all the ingredients except the white vinegar in a saucepan, cover, and simmer over low heat for about an hour or until the liquid is reduced to

about 1½ cups. Transfer the mixture to
a food processor or blender and purée.

Combine the purée and the white vinegar
in a bowl and mix thoroughly to the desired consistency. Strain the sauce through a sieve and discard the solids. Bottle in sterilized jars.

SALSA DE CHIPOTLE

(Chipotle Chile Sauce)

YIELD: ABOUT 2¹/₂ CUPS   HEAT SCALE: HOT

From Tlaxcala, Mexico comes a wonderful sauce that utilizes any type of smoked chile. Most commonly, they are smoked red jalapeños. This is a table sauce served at room temperature to spice up any main dish, including meats.

   10 dried chipotle chiles
   4 mulato chiles, or anchos
   ½ onion, chopped
   10 cloves garlic
   1 tablespoon sesame seeds
   10 black peppercorns
   10 cumin seeds
   ½ cinnamon stick
   1 teaspoon Mexican oregano
   ½ teaspoon salt
   2 tablespoons olive oil
   4 tablespoon vegetable oil

¼ cup vinegar
1 cup water

Soak all the chiles in hot water until soft, about 1 hour. Remove the seeds and stems.

In a food processor or blender, combine the chiles, onion, garlic, sesame seeds, peppercorns, cumin seeds, cinnamon stick, Mexican oregano, and salt and process to a paste.

Heat the olive oil and vegetable oil together in a saucepan and fry the paste over medium heat until it is aromatic, stirring constantly, for about 5 minutes. Add the vinegar and water, remove from the heat, and stir well.

CHIPOTLE-TOMATILLO SAUCE

YIELD: 4 CUPS   HEAT SCALE: MEDIUM

Ah, the smoky flavor of the chipotle—or is that a meco or morita, other types of smoked chiles? It won't matter for this sauce, because any smoked chile will work. If using dried chipotles, be sure to soak them first in water to soften them. This is a great sauce for grilled or barbecued meat.

    1 onion, chopped
    4 cloves garlic, chopped
    2 tablespoon vegetable oil
    1 pound tomatillos, halved
    1 large tomato, chopped
    ½ cup chicken broth
    ½ teaspoon Mexican oregano
    3 canned chipotle chiles en adobo
    1 teaspoon vinegar
    Salt to taste

In a skillet, sauté the onions and garlic in the oil until soft and slightly browned.

In a food processor or blender, combine all ingredients except the salt and purée. Transfer the purée to a skillet and simmer for 20 minutes to thicken slightly.

CHIPOTLE-CORN SALSA WITH POBLANOS AND MORELS

YIELD: 4 SERVINGS   HEAT SCALE: MILD

One of the tenets of New Southwestern cooking is the innovative combination of farm-fresh ingredients. This recipe, made with mostly New World foods, is a good example. Serve with roasted meats, such as mesquite-grilled quail.

  5 ears of corn in husks
  5 tablespoons diced morels (or other wild mushrooms)
  7 teaspoons olive oil
  2 poblano chiles, roasted, peeled, stems and seeds removed, diced
  ¼ cup sundried tomatoes, minced
  2 tablespoons minced cilantro
  1 tablespoon chipotles in adobo, minced
  2 teaspoons fresh marjoram, minced
  1 teaspoon lime juice
  Salt to taste

Place the corn on a baking sheet and bake at 400 degrees for 30 minutes, turning often, until the corn is blackened on all sides. Allow to cool.

Cook the morels in 2 teaspoons of the olive oil until well browned, about 10 minutes.

Shuck the corn and brush with 2 teaspoons of olive oil. Grill or broil the corn until the kernels brown, about 10 minutes. Cut the kernels from the cob and reserve.

Combine the corn and the morels with the remaining ingredients (and the remaining olive oil) and mix well. Serve warm on a bed of greens.

SMOKY MAYONNAISE

YIELD: 1 CUP   HEAT SCALE: MEDIUM

Use this interesting variation on mayonnaise whenever the bland kind is called for. It's especially good as a topping for cold, cooked shrimp and hard-boiled eggs or as a dip for raw vegetables.

2 chipotle chiles, rehydrated, seeds and stems removed, or 2 chipotle chiles in adobo sauce plus 2 teaspoons of adobo sauce
½ cup prepared mayonnaise
½ cup sour cream
¼ teaspoon dried cilantro flakes

In a blender or food processor, combine the rehydrated chipotles and 2 teaspoons of the rehydrating water and purée. Alternately, if using chipotles in adobo, purée the chipotles with 2 teaspoons of the sauce.

Add the puréed chipotles to the mayonnaise, sour cream, and cilantro flakes, and mix well.

SMOKY CHIPOTLE PESTO

YIELD: 2½ CUPS   HEAT SCALE: MEDIUM

From our friend J.P. Hayes of Sgt. Pepper's Hot Sauce Micro Brewery in Austin comes this excellent pesto designed to be served over pasta or as a pizza topping. Mix it with mayonnaise or ranch dressing and it's a tasty dip. J.P. gave a dramatic demonstration of preparing this pesto without electricity at the 1996 Texas Hill Country Wine and Food Festival.

    1 can chipotle chiles in adobo
    8 cloves garlic
    2 tablespoons cider vinegar or lime juice
    1 cup grated parmesan or romano cheese
    1 cup pumpkin seeds or pine nuts, toasted
    1 cup canola oil

Combine the chipotles, garlic, and vinegar in a food processor and purée. Add the cheese and pumpkin seeds and finely chop. With the processor running, drizzle in the oil until the desired consistency is reached (you may not need all the oil).

CHIPOTLE BLOODY MARIA

YIELD: 1 SERVING   HEAT SCALE: MEDIUM

Think this drink is just a bloody mary with tequila switched for the vodka? Well, almost. ¡Salud!

2 ounces tequila
3 ounces tomato juice
1½ teaspoons lime juice
Dash Worcestershire sauce
Dash celery salt
Dash black pepper
Dash salt
1½ teaspoons bottled chipotle hot sauce or Salsa de Chipotle (page 36)

Combine all ingredients and pour over ice.
Garnish with a slice of lime and serve.

Appetizers and breakfast

GUACAMOLE CON CHIPOTLE

YIELD: 4 SERVINGS HEAT SCALE: MEDIUM

Everyone's tried the usual guacamole dip, but not everyone has experienced it smoky-style, as in this recipe. Traditionally, it is served with tortilla chips, but other chips work equally well, including out favorite—plantain chips. Serve within 3 hours of making.

2 ripe Haas avocados, peeled and pitted
1 small white onion, minced
1 tomato, minced
1 tablespoon lime or lemon juice
2 chipotle chiles in adobo sauce, minced
Salt to taste

Combine all ingredients in a bowl and mix well. Cover and serve chilled.

CHIPOTLE CHILE DIP,
CORDOBESA-STYLE

YIELD: 10 TO 12 SERVINGS   HEAT SCALE: MEDIUM

Serve this with fresh vegetables of your choice. We particularly recommend carrot and celery sticks.

    4 cups water
    4 ounces dried chipotle chiles, stems and seeds
        removed
    1 cup packed brown sugar
    ½ teaspoon salt, plus salt to taste
    2 cups wine vinegar
    ⅓ cup olive oil
    4 onions, chopped
    1 head of garlic, sectioned
    ¼ teaspoon thyme
    ¼ teaspoon oregano
    1 cup sour cream
    1 cup mayonnaise
    1 tablespoon lemon juice

Place the water, chiles, brown sugar,
and salt to taste in a sauce pan and heat
on low until the chiles rehydrate and the peel
is easily loosened. Once the peels are removed,
add the vinegar. Remove the pan from the heat. In
another pan, combine the olive oil, onion, garlic, ½
teaspoon salt, thyme, and oregano and sauté until
the onions are soft. Puree the chiles in a blender,
along with two tablespoons of the liquid from the
saucepan.

In a bowl, mix together the puréed chiles, onion
mixture, sour cream, mayonnaise and lemon juice.

CHIPOTLE CHILAQUILES

Ah, we love the way the wonderful, smoky-hot flavor of the chipotle comes through in this breakfast classic. It can be baked or microwaved, but either way it takes only a few minutes to prepare.

    2 tomatoes, chopped
    4 chipotles in adobo, chopped
    2 cloves garlic, chopped
    ½ onion, chopped
    ½ cup vegetable stock
    Vegetable oil
    6 corn tortillas, cut into eighths
    4 eggs, beaten
    1 cup grated Monterey Jack or cheddar cheese
    Chopped cilantro, for garnish

Combine the tomatoes, chipotles, garlic, onion, and stock in a blender and purée to make a sauce.
Bring the sauce to a boil, reduce the heat, and simmer for 15 minutes or until the sauce is thickened.

Heat a couple of inches of oil in a pan. Fry each tortilla in the oil only for a few seconds a side until soft, remove and drain on paper towels.

Combine the sauce and eggs.

To assemble the casserole, line the bottom of a small casserole dish with tortilla wedges, then add ⅓ of the sauce mixture, and top with ⅓ of the cheese. Repeat twice more.

Bake the casserole in a 300 degree oven for 15 minutes, or microwave on high for about 5 minutes.

Garnish with the cilantro and serve.

CHIPOTLE SPOONBREAD

YIELD: 6 SERVINGS   HEAT SCALE: HOT

Dave's favorite spoonbread recipe features chipotles, and the heat level can be adjusted downwards, if desired. Dried chipotles can be used if they are soaked in hot water for 1 hour before puréeing.

2½ cups low-fat milk
1 cup yellow cornmeal
3 eggs (or egg substitute)
2 teaspoons sugar
½ teaspoon salt
4 tablespoons melted margarine
1 teaspoon thyme or marjoram
1 teaspoon baking powder
3 chipotle chiles, puréed without the adobo sauce
½ cup grated jalapeño cheese

Heat 2 cups of milk to simmering and stir in the cornmeal. When the mixture is thick, remove it from the heat.

Beat the eggs well and mix in the remaining ½

cup milk, the sugar, salt, and melted margarine. Combine with the hot corn-meal mixture. Stir in the thyme or marjoram, baking powder, and puréed chipotles. Mix thoroughly. Pour into a well-greased 1½ quart baking dish or casserole. Bake in a 400 degree oven for 45 minutes or until the spoon bread is firm and lightly browned. Spoon onto plates and serve at once.

SMOKED BEAN DIP

YIELD: 4 SERVINGS   HEAT SCALE: MEDIUM

Here's a smoky twist on refried beans that are used as a dip for chips or a filling for burritos or soft tacos.

    1 tablespoon vegetable oil
    ½ white onion, chopped
    4 cloves garlic, minced
    1 teaspoon cumin
    ½ teaspoon salt
    2 chipotle chiles in adobo, minced
    1 cup cooked pinto or black beans

Heat the oil in a skillet and add the onion and garlic and sauté until the onions are soft, about 5 minutes. Add the cumin, salt, and chipotles, and cook for about two minutes.

Purée the beans in a food processor with a little water until you have a smooth paste. Add the paste to the mixture in the skillet and cook for 2 minutes, stirring constantly.

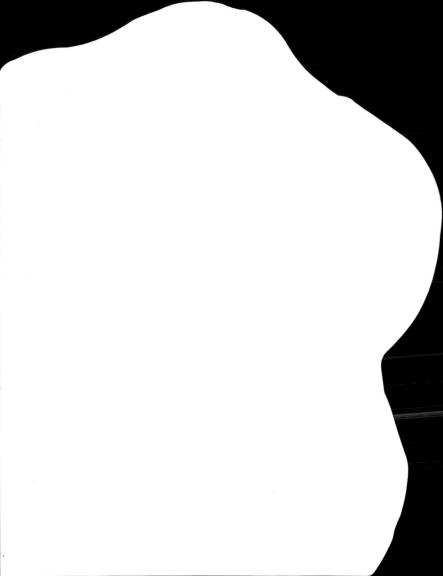

Soups and salads

SMOKIN' OYSTER SOUP

YIELD: 4 TO 6 SERVINGS   HEAT SCALE: MEDIUM

When Dave was in college, he made soups similar to this one to use up excess Chesapeake Bay oysters. Unfortunately, he had never heard of chipotles at that time, but always adds them now.

3 jars fresh oysters
1 quart chicken stock
1 cup white wine
5 chipotle chiles in adobo, chopped fine
1 white onion, chopped fine
4 slices bacon, shredded
4 slices ham, chopped

In a large pan, combine all the ingredients and simmer, uncovered, over medium heat, for 30 minutes. Add additional wine, if desired.

BLACK BEAN AND CHIPOTLE SOUP

YIELD: 6 TO 8 SERVINGS   HEAT SCALE: MEDIUM

There are many recipes for black bean soup, but this one is special. From Mary Jane Wilan, it's an amalgam of Cuban style, Panama style, and Southwest style.

1 pound dried black beans

1 green bell pepper, whole

⅔ cup olive oil

1 cup onion, diced

4 cloves garlic, finely chopped

1 green bell pepper, diced

½ teaspoon freshly ground black pepper

1 tablespoon dried oregano

1 bay leaf

2 tablespoons sugar

1 to 2 teaspoons ground cumin

1 large can (28 ounces) tomatoes, undrained

2 tablespoons New Mexican chile powder

2 tablespoons chopped cilantro

2 chipotle chiles in adobo sauce, minced

6 to 8 cups chicken or vegetable stock
2 tablespoons white vinegar
2 tablespoons white wine
2 tablespoons olive oil

Wash the beans and rinse thoroughly. Put them in a large, heavy pot with water to cover and the whole green bell pepper and bring to a boil. Lower the heat to a simmer and cook for about 2½ hours, or until the beans are almost tender.

Heat the olive oil in a sauté pan and add the onion, garlic, and diced bell pepper and sauté for 2 minutes, or until the pepper is softened. Add to the cooked beans, along with the pepper, oregano, bay leaf, sugar, cumin, tomatoes, chile powder, cilantro, and chipotles. Simmer slowly for about 45 minutes, adding the stock as needed. Add the vinegar, wine, and olive oil and simmer the beans for another 45 minutes, adding more vegetable stock if necessary.

CALDO TLALPEÑO

(Tlalpan Soup)

YIELD: 4 TO 6 SERVINGS   HEAT SCALE: MEDIUM

Here is a classic soup from central Mexico. The name comes from Tlalpan, which is a suburb of Mexico City. This soup takes a bit of time to cook, but it's well worth the effort. Substitute Chipotle Paste (page 32) for the canned chipotles, if desired.

3 cups chicken stock

1 quart water

1 cup corn, cut from the cob

2 carrots, peeled and sliced

2 summer squash, sliced

1 white onion, sliced

4 cloves garlic, chopped fine

3 chipotle chiles in adobo, chopped

4 boneless chicken breasts, cooked and shredded

4 sprigs cilantro, chopped

Salt and pepper

1 avocado

In a large pan, combine the stock,
water, corn, carrots, squash, onion, garlic,
and chipotles and simmer, uncovered, over
medium-low heat for ½ hour.

Add the chicken and cilantro and simmer,
uncovered, over medium-low heat for 1 hour. Add
salt and pepper to taste.

Serve with avocado slices in soup bowls.

JULIO'S SALPICÓN

YIELD: 12 SERVINGS   HEAT SCALE: MEDIUM

This is the famous shredded meat salad that is one of El Paso's most popular and unique dishes. It crossed the border because of Julio Ramirez, who opened his first restaurant in 1944 in Juárez and a second location in El Paso in 1985. The recipe for salpicón has been imitated and begged for, and local restaurateurs have paid hundreds of dollars to professional recipe testers to see if they could approximate the recipe. Finally, the Ramirez family has released it. Note that this recipe requires advance preparation.

3 pounds beef brisket
2 cloves garlic, minced
Salt to taste
1 cup diced white cheddar cheese
½ cup chopped cilantro
½ cup diced, seeded tomatoes
½ cup vegetable oil
½ cup wine vinegar

4 chipotle chiles in adobo, minced
Diced avocado for garnish

Bring the brisket to a boil in water to cover, with garlic and salt. Reduce heat and simmer for about 1 and ½ hours, uncovered, until the meat is tender and can be shredded. Cool the meat in the broth and then shred finely by hand. Reserve the broth to make a stew or soup.

Toss the shredded brisket with the remaining ingredients (except the avocado). Chill the mixture and allow it to marinate for a couple of hours or preferably overnight.

Line a platter with lettuce leaves, place the salpicón on the leaves, and garnish with the avocado. Serve with hot, buttered flour tortillas.

SOPA DE POLLO Y ARROZ
CON CHIPOTLES

(Rice and Chicken Soup with Chipotles)

YIELD: 4 TO 6 SERVINGS   HEAT SCALE: MEDIUM

If chicken soup is good for the soul, when spiced with chipotles it's great for the stomach as well.

3 quarts chicken broth
3 celery stalks, chopped
1 pound mushrooms, sliced
1 cup rice
4 chipotle chiles in adobo, chopped
2 chicken breasts, cooked and shredded
4 tablespoons lemon or lime juice
1 tablespoon dried cilantro flakes
2 tablespoons fresh dill

Bring the chicken broth to a boil and add the celery, mushrooms, rice, and chipotles. Reduce the heat and simmer, uncovered, for 45 minutes. Add the chicken, lemon or lime juice, cilantro, and dill and simmer for 10 minutes.

Main courses

JUMBO SHRIMP WITH SMOKED COCKTAIL SAUCE

YIELD: 8 SERVINGS   HEAT SCALE: MEDIUM

This recipe is so simple we're almost embarrassed to include it here. But it's such a tasty twist on the usual shrimp cocktail that we couldn't resist passing it on. The sauce is also great with steamed oysters and clams.

48 jumbo shrimp, cooked, and chilled
1 jar commercial cocktail sauce
¼ cup Chuck's Chipotle Sauce (page 34)

Arrange the shrimp attractively on a platter. In a bowl, combine the cocktail sauce and Chuck's Chipotle Sauce. Guests dip the shrimp in the newly energized cocktail sauce.

TOURNEDOS CHIPOTLE

YIELD: 4 SERVINGS   HEAT SCALE: HOT

We confess to smuggling Mexican recipes into the Southwest. Here is the preferred way to prepare steaks in Puerto Vallarta, a method we fell completely in love with during our visits there.

4 beef fillets, 1 to 2 inches thick
Olive oil
1 onion, chopped
3 cloves garlic, minced
2 tablespoons vegetable oil
3 canned chipotle chiles in adobo
1 tomato, peeled and seeds removed, chopped
½ teaspoon oregano
½ teaspoon sugar
½ teaspoon freshly ground black pepper
2 cups beef broth
1 cup dry red wine

Brush the steaks with olive oil and let sit while you prepare the sauce.

In a skillet, sauté the onion and garlic in the vegetable oil until the onion is browned. Add the chiles, tomato, oregano, sugar, and pepper. Sauté for an additional 2 or 3 minutes. Stir in the broth and wine and simmer for 20 to 30 minutes, or until the liquid is reduced by half.

Remove from the heat, purée the sauce in a blender until smooth, and then strain it. Return the sauce to the pan and keep warm until ready for serving.

Broil or grill the steaks to desired doneness.

To serve, place some of the sauce on a plate, place the steak on the sauce, and top with additional sauce.

CHIPOTLES RELLENOS
(STUFFED CHIPOTLES)

YIELD: 8 SERVINGS   HEAT SCALE: HOT

Yes, even chipotle chiles can be stuffed. Here we use a meat and cheese filling, but other ingredients, such as raisins, can be added. Chicken or shrimp can also be substituted for the beef or pork.

¼ cup vegetable oil
1 white onion, chopped
1 pound ground beef or pork
2 eggs, lightly beaten
4 cups shredded mixed Monterey jack and cheddar
    cheese
24 chipotle chiles in adobo
2 cups Pasta de Chipotle (page 32)

Preheat oven to 350 degrees. Heat the vegetable oil in a skillet and sauté the onion until soft, about 5 minutes. In a separate bowl, add the onion to the beef, add the eggs, and mix well.

Return the beef mixture to the skillet and sauté

until brown. Drain any excess fat from the meat.

Make a slit in each chile and remove the seeds. Spoon equal amounts of the meat mixture and cheese mixture into the slits. Place the stuffed chiles in a casserole dish and spoon over the chipotle paste. Bake for 15 minutes and serve hot.

ALBONDIGAS EN SALSA CHIPOTLE (CHIPOTLE MEATBALLS)

YIELD: 6 TO 8 SERVINGS   HEAT SCALE: MEDIUM

Here are simple meatballs in a vegetable chipotle sauce: one of Chuck's favorite smoky dishes.

4 chipotle chiles in adobo, finely chopped
2 small white onions, finely chopped
5 tomatoes, finely chopped
¼ cup finely chopped carrots
¼ cup finely chopped celery
¼ cup plus 2 tablespoons finely chopped cilantro
1 cup beef broth
1¼ teaspoons salt
1 teaspoon freshly ground black pepper
1 pound ground pork
1 pound ground beef
½ cup bread crumbs
½ cup milk
2 eggs

Preheat oven to 350 degrees. In a saucepan, combine the chiles, 1 of the chopped onions, tomatoes, carrots, celery, ¼ cup of the cilantro, the broth, ¼ teaspoon of the salt, and ½ teaspoon of the pepper and cook, uncovered, over medium heat for 10 minutes. Reduce the heat and simmer for 30 minutes.

While the sauce is cooking, combine the remaining ingredients, mix well, and fashion into meatballs. Bake the meatballs for 20 minutes. Remove, drain, and add them to the chipotle sauce. Simmer meatballs in the sauce for 20 minutes.

CHIPOTLE HOT WINGS

YIELD: 24 TO 30 PIECES   HEAT SCALE: MEDIUM

Here's a twist on Buffalo wings for lovers of all things smoky. However, we have remained somewhat traditional by serving it with Blue Cheese Dressing.

2½-pounds chicken wings (12 to 15 wings)
¼ cup Chuck's Chipotle Sauce (page 34)
1 teaspoon onion powder
1 teaspoon garlic powder
½ teaspoon dried thyme
½ teaspoon dried oregano
½ cup (1 stick) butter or margarine, melted

Split the wings at each joint and discard the tips. Wash the wing sections and pat dry. Deep fry at 400 degrees (high) for 12 minutes or until completely cooked and crispy, then drain.

Combine the hot sauce and spices with the melted butter in a small saucepan. Simmer for a couple of minutes to blend the flavors. Dip wings in the sauce to coat completely.

Blue Cheese Dressing

YIELD: ABOUT 1³/₄ CUPS

1 cup mayonnaise
2 tablespoons finely chopped onion
1 teaspoon finely minced garlic
¼ cup finely chopped parsley
½ cup sour cream
1 tablespoon lemon juice
1 tablespoon white vinegar
¼ cup crumbled blue cheese

Combine all ingredients and chill for one hour before serving.

PECHUGAS AL CHIPOTLE
(CHIPTOTLE CHICKEN BREASTS)

YIELD: 4 SERVINGS   HEAT SCALE: MEDIUM

Here's a no-brainer recipe that tastes like it's a lot more complicated than it is. Fish fillets may also be prepared in this manner.

¼ cup vegetable oil
1 white onion, chopped fine
4 boneless chicken breasts
½ cup Pasta de Chipotle (see recipe, p. 32)
2 cups sour cream
1 cup mixed grated Monterey jack and cheddar cheese
¼ cup chopped fresh cilantro
2 cups refried beans

Heat the oil in a skillet and sauté the onions until tender, about 5 minutes. Add the chicken breasts and fry on both sides until they are golden brown, about 7 minutes a side.

In a separate pan, combine the chipotle paste

and sour cream and cook over low heat, stirring occasionally, for 5 minutes.

Place each chicken breast on a plate, spoon the chipotle sauce over each, and top with the cheese mixture. Place each dish in the oven and heat until the cheese melts. Remove from the oven, garnish with the cilantro, and serve with heated refried beans.

ZACATECAN PAN-FRIED FISH WITH CHIPOTLE PASTE

YIELD: 4 TO 6 SERVINGS　　　　HEAT SCALE: MEDIUM

From the state of Zacatecas in Mexico comes this smoky fish recipe. Serve it with cole slaw and french fried potatoes. The fillets also make a great sandwich when served with Smoky Mayonnaise (page 42).

6 fillets firm white fish, such as cod or perch
½ cup lemon juice
Salt and pepper
Flour
2 eggs, beaten
½ cup vegetable oil
½ cup Pasta de Chipotle (see recipe, page 32)

Toss the fillets with the lemon juice and salt and pepper to taste and allow to marinate for 15 minutes.

Dip the fillets in the flour and then in the beaten egg mixture. Pan-fry the fillets in the vegetable oil until golden brown, about 5 to 6 minutes a side.

Remove and drain on paper towels.

Heat the chipotle paste and drizzle it over the fillets just before serving.

CHIPOTLE-CORN STUFFED
POBLANO CHILES

YIELD: 6 SERVINGS   HEAT SCALE: MEDIUM

Here's a classic vegetarian dish from the American Southwest that includes two chile flavors, plus two other native favorites—corn and pecans.

2 eggs
1½ cups cooked corn
½ cup chopped pecans
½ cup chopped red bell pepper
½ cup chopped onion
¼ cup Salsa de Chipotle (see recipe, page 36)
Salt and pepper to taste
6 poblano chiles, roasted, peeled, seeds and stems
     removed, and halved
Chopped fresh cilanto, for garnish

Preheat the oven to 375 degrees. Beat the eggs in a bowl for about 4 minutes, then stir in the remaining ingredients, except the poblanos.

Place the poblano halves in a greased baking

dish. Place about ¼ cup of the corn mixure in each half. Cover and bake for 25 minutes. Garnish with the cilantro.

SOUTHWESTERN
CHIPOTLE BAKED BEANS

YIELD: 6 SERVINGS   HEAT SCALE: HOT

Pinto beans are not the only variety served in the Southwest. Try these interesting great northern beans as a spicy side dish.

3 canned chipotle chiles in adobo, stems removed, chopped
1 large onion, chopped
2 cloves garlic, chopped
1 tablespoon vegetable oil
2 teaspoons ground red New Mexican chile
2 tablespoons adobo sauce (from the canned chiles)
¼ pound bacon, cut in ½ inch pieces
½ cup catsup
½ cup beer or water
¼ cup dark brown sugar
1 teaspoon dry mustard
3 cups cooked great northern beans

Sauté the chipotle chiles, onions, and garlic in the oil until soft.

Combine this mixture with the remaining ingredients in a baking dish.

Cover and bake the beans in a 325 degree oven for 2 hours or until the beans are tender and coated with the sauce. Add water if the mixture gets too dry.

MARINATED CHIPOTLE ZUCCHINI

YIELD: 8 SERVINGS   HEAT SCALE: MEDIUM

3 to 4 tablespoons olive oil
1 medium onion, cut in ¼-inch slices
4 small zucchini, cut lengthwise in half
1 tablespoon wine vinegar
1 canned chipotle in adobo, chopped
Chopped fresh cilantro or parsley

Heat the oil and sauté the onion until soft. Place the zucchini halves, cut-sides down, on top of the onion. Reduce the heat, cover the pan and cook for 20 minutes or until tender. Remove the vegetables and keep warm.

Stir the vinegar, chile, and the additional oil, if necessary. Simmer the marinade for a couple of minutes to blend the flavors.

Place the zucchini on a plate and top with the onions. Pour the marinade over the top and allow to marinate for 15 to 20 minutes.

Top with the chopped cilantro and serve either warm or at room temperature.

RESOURCES

Suggested reading

DeWitt, Dave and Chuck Evans. *The Hot Sauce Bible*. Freedom, CA: The Crossing Press, 1996.

DeWitt, Dave and Nancy Gerlach. *Just North of the Border*. Rocklin, CA: Prima Publishing, 1992.

DeWitt, Dave and Mary Jane Wilan and Melissa T. Stock. *Hot & Spicy Mexican*. Rocklin, CA: Prima Publishing, 1996.

McMahon, Jacqueline Higuera. *Chipotle Chile Cook Book*. Lake Hughes, CA: The Olive Press, 1994.

Mail-Order Sources

Chile Today-Hot Tamale
2-D Great Meadow Lane
East Hanover, NJ 07936
(800) 468-7377

Colorado Spice Company
5030 Nome St., Unit A
Denver, CO 80239
(303) 373-0141

Coyote Cocina
1364 Rufina Circle #1
Santa Fe, NM 87501
(800) 866-HOWL

Dean and DeLuca
Mail Order Department
560 Broadway
New York, NY 10012
(212) 431-1691

Enchanted Seeds
P.O. Box 6087
Las Cruces, NM 88006
(505) 233-3033

Flamingo Flats
Box 441
St. Michael's, MD 21663
(800) 468-8841

GMB Specialty Foods, Inc.
P.O. Box 962
San Juan Capistrano, CA 92693-0962
(714) 240-3053

Hot Sauce Club of America
P.O. Box 687
Indian Rocks Beach, FL 34635-0687
(800) Sauce-2-U

Hot Sauce Harry's
The Dallas Farmer's Market
3422 Flair Dr.
Dallas, TX 75229
(214) 902-8552

Le Saucier
Faneuil Hall Marketplace
Boston, MA 02109
(617) 227-9649

Melissa's World Variety Produce
P.O. Box 21127
Los Angeles, CA 90021
(800) 468-7111

Mo Hotta, Mo Betta
P.O. Box 4136
San Luis Obispo, CA 93403
(800) 462-3220

Old Southwest Trading Co.
P.O. Box 7545
Albuquerque, NM 87194
(505) 836-0168

Pendery's
304 East Belknap
Fort Worth, TX 76102
(800) 533-1879

Pepper Joe's, Inc.
7 Tyburn Ct.
Timonium, MD 21093
(410) 561-8158

Sauces & Salsas, Ltd.
1892 Rear Oakland Park Ave.
Columbus, OH 43224
(614) 268-7330

Shepherd Garden Seeds
6116 Highway 9
Felton, CA 95018
(408) 335-6910
South Side Pepper Co.
320 N. Walnut St.
Mechanicsburg, PA 17055

CONVERSIONS

Liquid

1 Tbsp = 15 ml

1/2 cup = 4 fl oz = 125 ml

1 cup = 8 fl oz = 250 ml

Dry

1/4 cup = 4 Tbsp = 2 oz = 60 g

1 cup = 1/2 pound = 8 oz = 250 g

Flour

1/2 cup = 60 g

1 cup = 4 oz = 125 g

Temperature

400° F = 200° C = gas mark 6

375° F = 190° C = gas mark 5

350° F = 175° C = gas mark 4

Miscellaneous

2 Tbsp butter = 1 oz = 30 g

1 inch = 2.5 cm

all-purpose flour = plain flour

baking soda = bicarbonate of soda

brown sugar = demerara sugar
confectioners' sugar = icing sugar
heavy cream = double cream
molasses = black treacle
raisins = sultanas
rolled oats = oat flakes
semisweet chocolate = plain chocolate
sugar = caster sugar

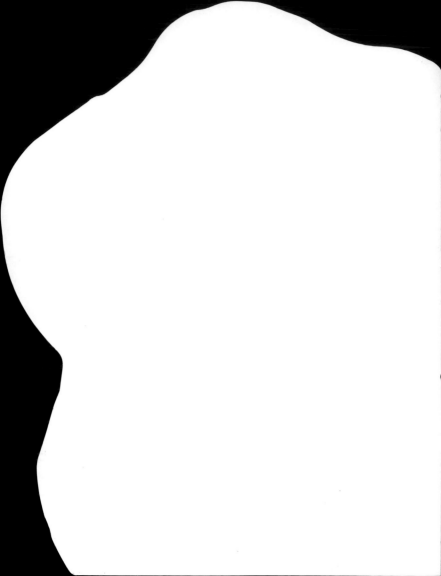